Common Sense
RETIREMENT

Common Sense Retirement: How To Get MORE From Your Retirement Plan

Published by Money Management Books, PMB 98, 2200 Kings Highway 3-L, Port Charlotte, FL 33980.

The author and publisher have made every effort to ensure the accuracy and completeness of the information contained in this book, however, we assume no responsibility for errors, inaccuracies, omissions, or any inconsistency herein. Names used are not intended to represent specific persons.

Library of Congress Control Number: 2004090018

Pelley, Paul W.
Common Sense Retirement: How To Get MORE From Your Retirement Plan
SUMMARY: Teaches how retirement plans work and how to manage mutual funds as you get ready to retire and throughout your retirement.

ISBN 0-9748088-0-6

First Edition

Common Sense
RETIREMENT

How To Get MORE
From Your Retirement Plan

By Paul W. Pelley, CFP®

Money Management Books
Florida

Acknowledgments

This book would not have been possible without the skills and insight of Christian Andersen who created the Multimedia CD-ROM which is an integral part of this book. Christian's patience and understanding were essential in helping put the material in an easy to understand, workable presentation. He can be reached at www.a-dcreations.com.

A special thank you to Erika True and Marilynn Peeke for their copy editing skills and organizational ability. They were instrumental in taking ideas and topics and putting them in an easy to read, logical format.

I sincerely appreciate the efforts and skills of Toya Koch in putting the manuscript and illustrations together. Her willing attitude to make changes and her skill at the computer made this an easy task. She can be contacted at toyshop@myactv.net.

Bill Kirstein's artistic skills for the cover design and his patience with making changes were monumental. I appreciate working with him.

Dedication

This book is dedicated to my family.
My wife, Gail, for her enthusiasm and
belief that this book would be possible.
My children, Amy and Paul who are
using the principles in this book to plan
their own retirement.

Note to the Reader

My objective in writing this book is to help you understand enough about your retirement plan, mutual funds and retirement to make good decisions about managing your retirement money.

This book answers questions asked by thousands of individuals in formal presentations and in individual meetings which I have conducted over the past 10 years. It is the simple essence of how our retirement "stuff" works.

Some sample comments made to me after a presentation: "I've been putting money in my retirement plan at work for over 20 years and this is the first time it made sense to me."

"My wife and I have been going to financial meetings for 10 years and these things have never been explained in such a simple and understandable way."

Some people have problems reading chapters with lots of numbers – their brains go fuzzy. Not to worry.

The enclosed Multimedia CD-ROM will actually show you the numbers and the way they flow. You can see and hear how it works. See page 102 for details.

Table of Contents

Preface

This book is for people who don't understand what to do with the money they have invested in their retirement plans.

"I don't understand the stock market."

"I just lost a lot of money."

"I keep putting in money every payday and my balance keeps going down."

"Am I in the 'best' mutual funds?"

"I'm going to retire in 5 years. What should I do?"

These are comments and questions I hear every day.

The following is a simple guide to understanding what is going on with your money and how you can increase your chances for a successful retirement.

This book is not an in-depth study about investing. Most retirement plans have detailed information about the concepts and terms discussed here. I encourage you to review their literature and visit their websites to learn more.

This book is a simple explanation of what goes on with your money in your mutual funds and how your retirement plan works.

"Common Sense Retirement: How To Get More From Your Retirement Plan" covers three sets of emotions in the human makeup. I am not a psychologist, but as an observer of human nature I've noticed three sets of emotions which I personally have experienced in regard to my investments. I am certain you will also identify with each one.

Chapter 1

Three Sets of Emotions

Fight or Flight

The first set of emotions investors encounter is "Fight or Flight." You get your retirement plan statements in the mail and you are afraid to open them. Some people throw them into a drawer and others throw them into the trash can.

I once met with a client and asked to see her statements. She handed me a stack of envelopes neatly wrapped with a rubber band. Not one of them had been opened! She told me that she was afraid to look at them because she knew that the market was down and she did not want to see the bad news. She was in "flight."

Others may put up a fight and open their statements but not know how to read them. As they look at their balances, questions pop into their minds. "Am I doing the right thing? Should I be making any changes?"

The financial media uses dramatic language to express their impression of what is happening in the market. They use words that create pictures in our minds – words like *"soar"* and *"plunge."* When you listen to the news or read the paper, try to read past the words used to sell the story and remember that the market will always continue to go up and down.

You can generally replace panic with control if you understand what is happening.

Fear and Greed

The next set of emotions is "Fear and Greed."

Once I met with a couple in their early 40's. They were concerned about the "beating" they were taking in the market. The balance in their investments had gone down almost 50%. They asked me whether the market could come back up before they retired. I asked them if they had made any changes in their mutual funds. They both indicated that they had been in the same funds for the last 10 years and had not made any changes. We discussed the fact that *they still had their shares* and that *they did have time* before they retired to watch for the market to come back up.

If you follow the news, you will see the market moving up and down daily. When you look closer you will find that world events like wars can cause the market to fall and news of peace can cause the market to rise.

I believe that the market is driven by *human nature*. Two fundamental aspects of human nature which I believe will be around as long as men and women walk on the earth are fear and greed.

You turn on the news and hear that the economy is heading toward a recession. Fear kicks in, people start worrying about their investments, and the market starts down. *What you say is what you get* — the recession shows up. Some time later the news tells us that the economy is getting better. People who paid $100 per share for a stock that is now $50 will repurchase those shares and get 2 for 1. Greed kicks in. Prices are low and the frenzied bidding for shares drives the prices back up. *Fear drives the prices down and greed drives them up*. I believe that human nature will not change. There will always be fear and greed.

Buy Low-Sell High

The third basic instinct is *buy low-sell high* which will be discussed later in the book.

The African Farmer

I am often asked about where the market will be in the future and I am reminded of an African farmer.

Some time ago I watched a television show about a family of rice farmers in Africa. They had a 4-acre plot in the flood plain of a river and planted rice there during the rainy season. The mother and father were working every day breaking up clods of dirt while waiting for the rain to start. The parents built a little hut to live by the river so they could be close to their land. The film then flashed back to a scene in their village which was miles away. The commentator indicated that the grandparents were watching their five grandchildren so they could attend school in the village. The children were attending the local school because the parents were committed to creating a better life for their children.

When I am asked about the future and if the market will come back I think of this story. As long as there are parents and as long as they want more for their children than what they have – the market will go up. We just don't know *when*.

Chapter 2

CD How Do Mutual Funds Work?

Let's say I meet with each employee where you work and ask them to give me $10 every payday so I can invest that money in large companies for them. If there were 1000 employees, I would get $10 from each of the 1000 employees which would be $10,000 ($10 x 1000) every payday.

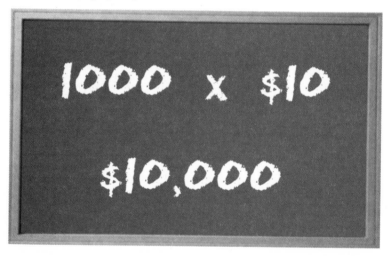

The first payday I received the $10,000 I might buy stock in IBM, the second payday perhaps stock in AT&T, the third payday WALMART stock, and the fourth payday I could purchase stock in Home Depot. I am buying stock in large companies for the *mutual* benefit of the employees. This is why they are called *mutual funds.*

A mutual fund allows you to put a small amount of your paycheck ($10) with other people's paychecks (1000) to send a big check ($10,000) to a professional fund manager. That fund manager has a research department to figure out what stocks to buy and sell.

You personally have made two decisions. First, you decided to put in $10 each payday and, second, you decided to put that money in large companies.

Most retirement plans today have mutual funds. Choosing which funds to invest in is not easy since there are over 10,000 mutual funds. We will cover investing in Chapter 11.

Chapter 3

(CD) How You Buy Mutual Funds

Let's assume you were to invest $100 each payday into a mutual fund and the first time it cost you $100 a share, how many shares would you buy? One – you invested $100 and it cost $100 so you would get 1 share.

$100/payday -- mutual fund

$100 -- 1 share

However, the next payday the share price drops to $50 per share. Now you would be buying 2 shares.

The next payday the price drops to $25 per share so you would be buying 4 shares.

The next payday the price drops to $20 per share and you would receive 5 shares.

$100/payday -- mutual fund

$100 -- 1 share

$50 -- 2 shares

$25 -- 4 shares

$20 -- 5 shares

This is what you did. You invested $100 for 4 paydays for a total of $400 dollars. You bought 1 plus 2 plus 4 plus 5 shares for a total of 12 shares.

$100/payday -- mutual fund

$100 -- 1 share $100

$50 -- 2 shares $200

$25 -- 4 shares $300

$20 -- 5 shares $400

12 shares

I was working with a client named June who told me that every time she received her retirement plan statement she had less money than the previous statement. She was losing money even though she was

17

putting money in each payday. If this trend continued she was afraid that she wouldn't have any money for retirement. So she took all of the money she had in mutual funds and moved it to a Guaranteed Interest Account.

The market was down when she took the money out of her mutual funds. She took her 12 shares and sold them for $20 per share for a total of $240 (12 shares x $20). She paid $400 to buy the shares and then sold them for $240. She actually lost $160 the day she moved the money.

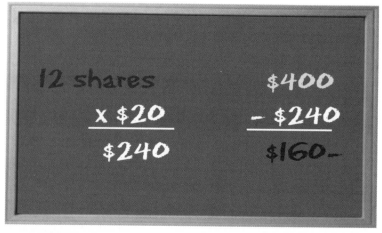

When I asked her how long it would be before she retired, she told me 25 years. What would happen if some time in the next 25 years (I cannot predict when) the market were to go back up to $100 a share?

The reason I'm willing to say the market could go back up to $100 per share is based on the past performance of the market.

No one can predict the future. I cannot tell you what will happen tomorrow. However, I can tell you exactly what has happened in the past. Since its inception, the market has averaged a 10% return. This means that every time the market went down, it had to come back up higher than it was before resulting in an upward trend.

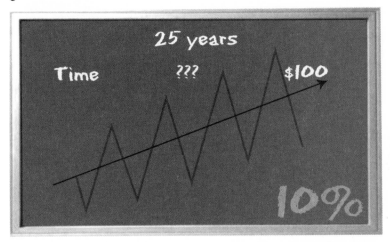

In my example, I am assuming that the market only comes back to where it was at the time of the first payday – not 10% higher. When the market comes back to $100 per share, June would have the potential to sell her 12 shares for a total of $1200 (12 shares x $100).

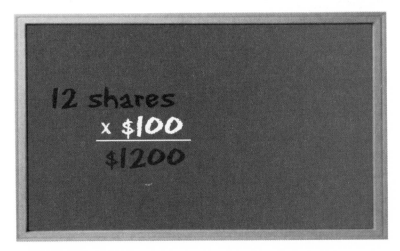

After her investment of $400 she could have a gain of $800 instead of a $160 loss. The difference between the gain and the loss is a *decision*.

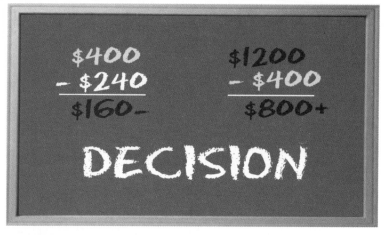

June told me the reason she decided to move her money out of the mutual funds and into a Guaranteed Interest Account was because every time she received her statement, the balance kept going down. After we finished speaking she understood that the most important number on her statement was *not her balance* but the *number of shares she owned*.

Buy as many shares as you can

Every payday when you put money into your retirement plan you are buying shares in mutual funds. Your test question is this: Can you buy more shares when the market is up or when the market is down? The answer is "down." You buy more shares when the market is down and the prices are low. While you are working you want to buy as many shares as you can. When you get ready to retire, you want to sell them for as much as you can. Have you ever heard of *buy low-sell high*?

Once you start investing in mutual funds you are riding a financial roller coaster. When you get ready to retire you need to have a way to get off at the top – to sell high.

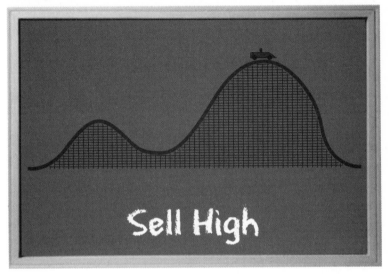

Chapter 4

(CD) How Do You Keep Track of The Highest Price?

In order to sell high, you need to know the highest prices you paid for your mutual fund shares. The easiest way to keep track of this is to put your statements in a notebook with one sheet of paper I call the **Highest Price** sheet.

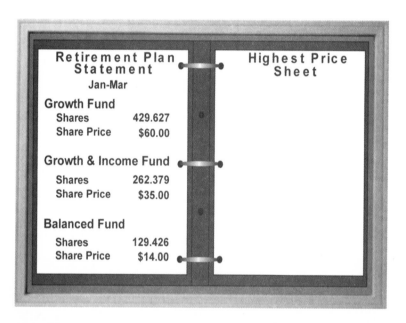

First, list each of your mutual funds on the Highest Price sheet. Then, every time you get a new statement, put it in your notebook.

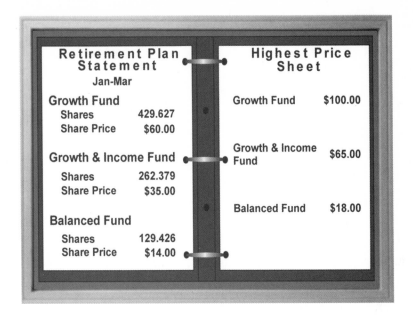

Then compare your new prices with the highest prices on your Highest Price sheet. As long as the new prices are lower than the highest prices, you bought more shares that quarter. The one number on your statement which is always increasing is the number of shares you have. You are always buying.

As an example, if the highest price you paid was $100 per share and the current price is $50 per share you purchased twice as many shares for the same amount of money. However, if the share price for one of your funds on your new statement is higher than the share price on your Highest Price sheet, scratch through the old price and write in the new price in order to keep track of the highest price.

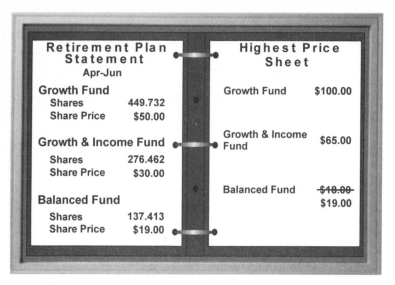

Retirement Plan Statement
Apr-Jun

Growth Fund
Shares — 449.732
Share Price — $50.00

Growth & Income Fund
Shares — 276.462
Share Price — $30.00

Balanced Fund
Shares — 137.413
Share Price — $19.00

Highest Price Sheet

Growth Fund — $100.00

Growth & Income Fund — $65.00

Balanced Fund — ~~$18.00~~ $19.00

The reason for keeping track of the highest price is so you can sell each of your shares for as much as possible. If you *sell high* you will increase your chances of having more money.

Three to five years before retirement

To make this work, you must allow enough time before you retire to start watching for the highest prices. Three to five years before retirement, start checking your share prices daily because you are getting ready to sell. When one of your funds reaches the highest price, move some of the money from that fund into the Guaranteed Interest Account (which I call my stash).

Build up a stash of cash

Before you retire, you should build up a stash of cash so as not to be forced to sell low. I personally have chosen to put three years worth of money into my stash.

Since everyone's financial situation is different, you may choose to have more or less than three years in your stash.

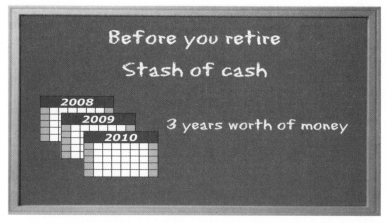

To calculate a stash amount, first estimate your retirement budget. Be sure to include all income sources as well as anticipated expenses. For income, you may have Social Security, pension, or real estate rentals. For expenses, include things such as a car, housing, medical expenses, travel, and charity.

Let's say that after calculating your budget you find yourself $500 a month short.

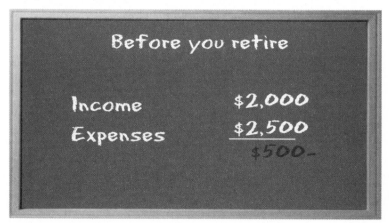

You have saved money in your retirement plan to make up for this shortfall – so you can do what you want during retirement! Three years is 36 months times $500 so you will need to put $18,000 (36 months x $500) in the Guaranteed Interest Account.

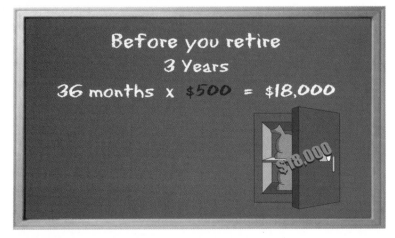

Three or four or five years before retirement, start watching your share prices. When one of your mutual funds reaches its highest price on your Highest Price sheet, move some money from that fund to your stash.

A year later another fund may go to its highest price. Then take some money from that fund for your stash. Keep selling high until you reach your goal of $18,000 in the Guaranteed Interest Account. Stop selling shares and wait until you retire.

After you retire, call your retirement plan company and ask them to start sending you $500 a month from the Guaranteed Interest Account.

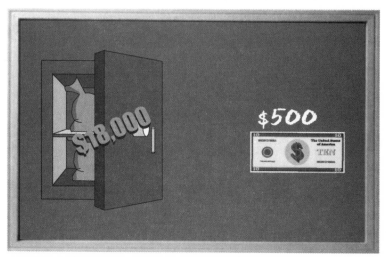

27

As you start taking money from your stash, continue to watch your share prices daily. When another one of your funds hits its highest price, you can move money from that fund into your stash.

What you are doing is **managing your money in retirement.** You are controlling when you sell so you can increase your chances of selling high. **Time is the only variable you can control.** You cannot control share prices. You must use time to watch in order to sell high.

The key to this whole process is to know how much you paid and to control when you sell.

Sell me your house

The other day I was discussing with a friend the importance of keeping track of the highest price I paid for my mutual fund shares. To illustrate this, I asked him if he owned a home. He told me he was making payments on his house and that the original price was $75,000. I told him that I would be willing to give him a check for $50,000 if he would sell me his home that day. He looked at me as if I was crazy and said that he had been living there for ten years and that his house was worth over $100,000. I then explained to him that one of these days he could have hundreds of thousands of dollars in his retirement plan. If he did not keep track of the highest price he paid for his shares he would not know what to sell them for when he retired. Think about it! You know how much you paid for your house *– do you know how much you paid for your shares?*

How can I find out my Highest Prices?

The easiest way to find out the highest prices you paid is to contact the account representative for your plan and ask for the highest prices. If you have a plan that does not offer the services of a local representative get out your old statements and look for the prices on them. The share price may be called unit value or unit price. Some companies refer to the number of shares as units or accumulation units.

After you have figured out where the information is on your statements, it's time to clean off the dining room table. Start at one end of the table and put your most recent statement at the corner. Line up your statements with the next most recent until you have them around the table. Now start looking for a specific fund and its price on each statement. Keep checking the prices until you find the highest. Write that price down on your Highest Price sheet next to the fund name. Continue the process until you have highest prices for all of your funds.

Some retirement account statements do not show your shares or share prices. In that instance, the best way to get your highest prices is to use the retirement plan website. After you set up your account access with a password, you can go to account detail or account transactions to see a history of your contributions.

Look at each contribution you made and determine the highest price you paid for your shares. Write that number on your Highest Price sheet. Repeat the same process for each of your funds. When you are finished you have your Highest Price sheet!

Why can't I wait until I retire to get the highest price?

You can wait! However, by keeping track of the highest price each time you get your statement, you can learn how to relate the prices and their changes to what is going on in the economy. When you listen to the news and hear that large companies are not doing well, you will see your statement reflect that news with lower share prices. Follow the market with your statements. Notice that your funds react differently depending on the trends in the economy. As you begin to have a better understanding of what is going on, you can have more confidence in managing your money for retirement.

The key to understanding is to know how something works.

The other day I had a nurse tell me she did not understand the stock market and was confused about how it works. Jokingly, of course, I asked her if I could give her a flu shot. When she discovered that I had never given anyone a shot before, she politely declined. However, if someone showed me how to give a shot, and I practiced, I think I could become quite good at it.

Just because you don't understand something doesn't mean that you cannot learn about it. The stock market is complex. If you break it down into small pieces and then practice, you can learn how to manage your money for retirement.

Chapter 5

How Many Years Until You Retire?

Several years ago, an associate told me about one of her clients who worked for Caterpillar, a manufacturer of large earth-moving equipment. Her client worked for them for 40 years and was getting ready to retire.

At 62, Don had $400,000 in his 401(k) which was all invested in Caterpillar stock. At that same time, Caterpillar stock was at an all time high. However, when Don turned 65, his account value was $200,000. The price of his stock had dropped by 50%. He came to her and wanted to buy secure investments so he could be sure that his money would be there when he needed it. He sold his shares of stock in Caterpillar and received $200,000 which he invested in bonds and Certificates of Deposit.

Don could have handled this situation much differently. When he was 62, he knew he would retire at 65. If he had sold some of his shares at the highest price when he was 62 and put, for example, $40,000 in a Guaranteed Interest Account for his stash, he would not have had to sell any of his shares at 65. He could have lived 2 or 3 years from his stash. That would have allowed the price of his Caterpillar stock a chance to come back up. As the stock price increased he would be using fewer and fewer shares to get the same amount of money.

If the market is down, nobody can predict when the price will come back up. Your stash buys you time for the market to come back up.

I'm 50 – what should I do?

Most people will not have enough money for retirement. When someone who is 50 years old asks me how much they need to save, the answer can be scary: You need to save more than you can afford. This situation does not mean you need to panic, but it does make sense to focus on the things you can do.

First, increase your contribution every time you get a raise. Next, review your investment choices – you may be invested too conservatively. And finally, set realistic goals for your retirement. A second home at the beach may have to give way to working part-time after you retire.

Today's economy is forcing the definition of retirement to change. Our grandparents retired with a pension and sat on the front porch watching the clouds go by. Most of us will not have a pension which pays us a guaranteed monthly income. For us, retirement may mean changing from full time work to part time, picking hobbies that could create income, or setting new goals to match the retirement funds we will have saved.

I am 60 – what should I do?

Everyone's financial situation is different. If you are 60 years old and all of your money is invested in mutual funds, what should you do if the market has been down for several years?

If you already have money in a Guaranteed Interest Account, calculate how long it will last after you retire. Use your retirement budget to help you see how long this would last.

If you need more money in your stash consider changing your future investments and putting your contributions directly into the Guaranteed Interest Account. You will be building up your stash of cash.

Think of it like this – if you start putting money into the Guaranteed Interest Account at age 60, you are buying time for the market to come back up. At 60 you have five years (from 60 to 65) before you would have to sell any of your shares. You have allowed 5 years for the market to come back up. *Time is on your side and it allows you to control when you sell.*

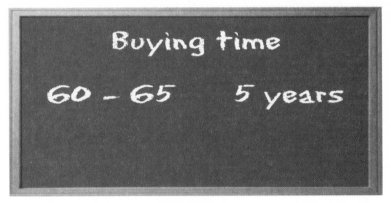

I'm 65 – what should I do?

Now you are 65. You have your stash and you retire. If you have 3 years worth of money in your stash you would not have to sell any shares for 3 years (from 65 to 68).

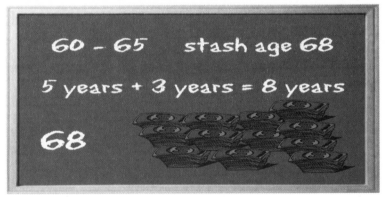

So from 60 to 68 you have not had to sell a single share. You have *eight* (5 + 3) years to wait for the market to come back up to your highest price.

I'm 68 – what should I do?

At 68 years of age you might have used up your stash of cash. You are going to be forced to sell some of your shares. Take out your notebook and open it to the Highest Price sheet.

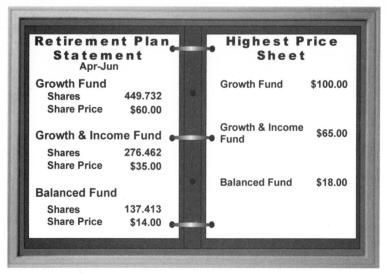

Get your current prices by going online to your retirement plan web site, calling their toll free number or checking the newspaper. Find the current prices of your mutual fund shares and compare them with your highest prices.

Let's say you have three funds and the Highest Price for your Growth Fund is $100 and the current price is $60. You would lose $40 per share if you sold shares from that fund ($100 - $60 = $40).

Your Growth and Income Fund has a highest price of $65 and the current price is $35 ($65 - $35 = $30). You would lose $30 per share. The highest price for your Balanced Fund was $18 and the current price is $14 ($18 - $14 = $4). You would lose $4 per share.

Which one should you sell? You would sell the Balanced Fund, which would minimize your loss. You would lose only $4 per share.

By keeping your Highest Price sheet you have a method of knowing which fund to sell to minimize your loss.

Chapter 6

ⒸⒹ How Much Money Am I Losing?

For this example, you are putting $10 each month into your retirement plan. The share price in January is $2 so you would have purchased 5 shares.

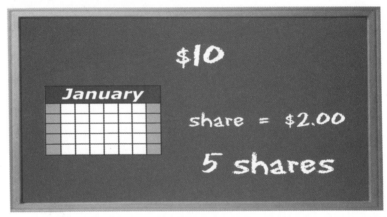

Next month in February, the market is up and the share price goes to $5. You would buy 2 shares.

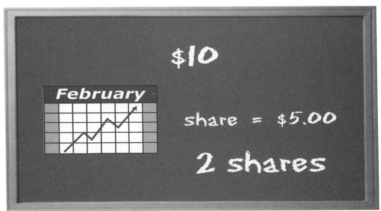

Then in March the price drops to $1 per share, so your $10 gets you 10 shares.

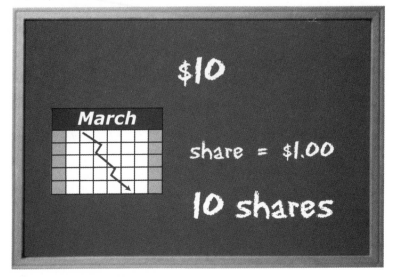

To think of it another way, you are going to the store each month with a $10 bill to buy bread. In January, the price is $2 a loaf so you would get 5 loaves. In February, the price is $5 a loaf so you could only buy 2 loaves and in March you would get 10 loaves since they are only $1 each.

During those three months you contributed a total of $30 into your retirement plan and purchased a total of 17 (5 + 2 + 10) shares. The highest price you paid was $5 per share. If you decide to wait until retirement and sell your 17 shares for $5 each you would receive $85 (17 shares x $5) – not bad for a $30 contribution.

$$\$30$$
$$5+2+10 = 17 \text{ shares}$$
$$\$5.00/\text{share}$$

$$17 \times \$5.00 = \$85.00$$

However, if you do not pay attention to the highest price you paid and decide to sell at the March price of $1 per share, you would only receive a check for $17 (17 shares x $1).

$$\$30$$
$$5+2+10 = 17 \text{ shares}$$
$$\$1.00/\text{share}$$

$$17 \times \$1.00 = \$17.00$$

Keeping track of the highest price could mean more money for your retirement.

41

Consider it your objective to buy as many shares as possible while you are working and then sell them for as much as possible. *Remember you are buying. The lower the price, the more shares you are getting for your money.*

Chapter 7

(CD) How a Statement is Made

In the previous example, you were putting $10 each month into your retirement plan. At the end of March, which is the end of the first quarter, the share price was $1. You purchased 17 shares during the quarter so your balance at the end of the quarter is $17 – the ending share price of $1 times the 17 shares you purchased during the quarter.

Jan	$10	$2/share	5 shares
Feb	$10	$5/share	2 shares
Mar	$10	$1/share	10 shares
			17 shares

$$\begin{array}{r} 17 \text{ shares} \\ \times\ \$1/\text{share} \\ \hline \$17 \end{array}$$

This balance may be upsetting to you because it looks as though you have lost money. You invested $30 and at the end of the quarter your investment is worth only $17. Your statement balance shows a loss of $13-.

```
Jan    $10    $2/share    5 shares

Feb    $10    $5/share    2 shares

Mar    $10    $1/share    10 shares
       $30                17 shares

              $30
              $17
              $13 -
```

However, as long as you do not sell your shares, your money is not lost. The only way you would lose your money would be if you panicked and transferred or moved your money into a new fund.

```
Jan    $10    $2/share    5 shares

Feb    $10    $5/share    2 shares

Mar    $10    $1/share    10 shares
       $30                17 shares


Move or transfer = sell = lost
```

When you see a minus sign next to your ending share balance, it really means that the price at the end of the quarter was lower than the price at the beginning of the quarter. You were actually able to buy more shares during that quarter.

Jan	$10	$2/share	5 shares
Feb	$10	$5/share	2 shares
Mar	$10	$1/share	10 shares
	$30		17 shares

If price is lower at end of quarter,
you bought more shares

Do you love to shop?

I find that the people who are most successful at understanding the market are people who love to shop. When the market is down everything is on sale.

Picture yourself at your favorite department store where you just found a really nice suit. The price tag shows that it is $300. Your budget says "no" but your heart says "yes," so you decide to look around some more. On a sales rack in the corner you spot the same item marked down to $60. You show both suits to the sales clerk and she tells you that both prices are correct. You pay her the $300 and take your new suit home. Right? Wrong! You pay the $60 and

45

the next day at work you tell everyone who admires your suit what a good shopper you are and how you found a great bargain. ***When the market is down – bargains abound.***

Do you own a dog?

One time I was speaking with clients who were worried about how the market kept going down. I asked them if they had any pets and they said that they had a dog. I then asked them how much they paid for dog food and they said $10 a bag.

"If you went to the pet store and found your regular dog food priced three bags for $10, would you only buy one bag?" They told me that of course they would buy three bags!

When the market is down you are buying more bags. Remember that while you are working, you are constantly buying shares.

Chapter 8

(CD) What is Dollar Cost Averaging?

Let's go back to the example of contributing $10 each month into your retirement plan. During the quarter you invested $30 and bought 17 shares. If you had waited until March when the cost per share was $1 and made your contribution of $30, you would have purchased 30 shares.

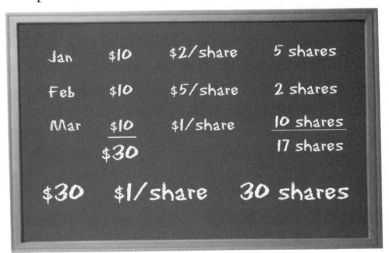

Jan	$10	$2/share	5 shares
Feb	$10	$5/share	2 shares
Mar	$10	$1/share	10 shares
	$30		17 shares
$30		$1/share	30 shares

By putting in $10 every month you actually bought more shares than if you had put all of the money in January or in February. If you had contributed the $30 in January you would have purchased 15 shares at $2 per share. In February your $30 would have purchased 6 shares at $5 each. By the end of March you actually ended up with 17 shares.

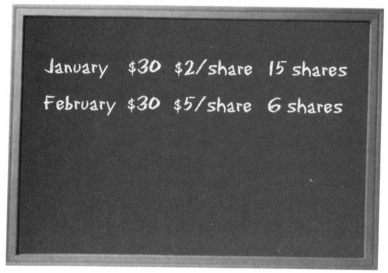

January $30 $2/share 15 shares

February $30 $5/share 6 shares

If you had waited to buy until the shares were $1 you would have done what is called *market timing*. Studies show that market timing works about 2% of the time. Your odds are better in Las Vegas. So if you want to lose money take a trip to Las Vegas – at least you can have a good time while you are losing it.

If the share price was $5 at the end of the quarter, your ending balance would be 17 shares times $5 or $85. Your ending balance is calculated by multiplying the number of shares at the end of the quarter times the ending share price.

When the share price is down it **looks** like you have lost money. However, if the share price is up it **looks** like you have made money. Either way you are still working and buying more shares.

You are *dollar cost averaging* when your contribution is automatically sent to your retirement plan every payday. *You are buying every payday.*

National Public Radio

When I travel, I listen to the Market Report on National Public Radio. When the news commentator says that the market is down 120 points, I hope that my employer sends my contribution to my retirement plan company that day.

You get the point: you are buying, and if the price is down you just got more for your money. ***Be a shopper.***

Chapter 9

You Are Accumulating Shares

The reason I focus on buying low and selling high is to help you understand that the assets you are accumulating are your shares – not your balance. When you get your statement in the mail, the first thing people tend to look at is their balance. If I had my way, I would not print the balance on statements. Your balance changes every day because the prices change every day. Your number of shares, however, is always increasing because you are buying more of them every payday.

It is possible to be accumulating shares even though you are not contributing to a mutual fund. For instance, if you have a retirement plan with a former employer and your money is in mutual funds, you may be accumulating shares. Here's why. Every month or quarter your funds may generate dividends or interest which is added to your account. When that money is put into your account, your fund manager purchases shares for you using the dividends or interest. You are getting more shares even though you are not making any additional contributions to that fund.

About 25 years ago, I invested $2,000 into a traditional IRA for three years in a row. I contributed a total of $6,000 and each time I made a contribution I purchased shares. I have not contributed any more money to my IRA, but today it is worth over $25,000. Over the years the dividends and interest have purchased more shares and inflation has made the shares worth more. If I were to sell my shares at their highest price, I could have over $35,000. I am making the decision to wait.

Let's go on a cruise

My wife and I are retired and we want to go on a cruise. The cost of the cruise is $5000.

I have been watching my share prices and one of my mutual funds has come up to the highest price I paid which was $100 per share. Since my fund is at its highest price, I call up my retirement plan company and ask them to send me $5000 from that fund. They calculate that at $100 per share it will take 50 shares to get me $5000 ($100 x 50 shares). They sell the 50 shares and I get my check for the cruise.

Let's say I've not paid any attention to my share prices and I decide to call my retirement plan and ask them to send me the $5000. The day I call, the price is $50 per share. At the end of the day they calculate that it will take 100 shares to get my $5000 ($50 x 100 shares). Which is better – to use 50 shares or 100 shares to go on the cruise?

Using 50 shares for a cruise is the better choice. By watching my share prices I could have the opportunity to go on an additional cruise.

For retirement, the most precious things I own are the shares I've purchased. When I sell one of them it is gone forever. I want to get the most money I possibly can for each of my shares. When I stop working, my contributions to my retirement plan stop and I am no longer actively buying shares. The shares I own must last me for the rest of my life. *My balance is not my asset – my shares are.*

What is the average share cost?

Let's say the market is going down. At one time one of your mutual fund's highest share price was $120. The current price is now $20 per share.

You'd probably feel as though you'd just lost a lot of money? You'd want to get out *NOW!* However, instead of getting out of this fund which, by the way, is invested in science and technology, you continue buying shares. You can now get 6 times as many shares as you were able to buy before.

As you accumulate more and more shares your cost per share is going lower and lower. You bought shares as the price was going up to the highest price and you are continuing to buy shares as the price is going down. You have to make a fundamental decision that science and technology will be around when you retire. Will science and technology continue to exist? If your answer is yes – keep buying.

Most people panic when they find their share prices low. They sell their shares and actually lose money. By continuing to purchase shares, you are dropping your average share cost. Once the market turns around and starts going up you can break even and then start to make money.

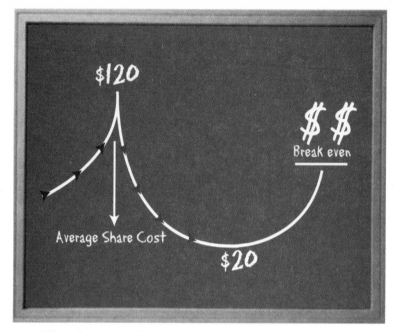

If a fund really makes you nervous, you could reduce the amount you are contributing to that fund by *changing your future investment percentages.*

Chapter 10

The Sell High Model
The 3rd Basic Instinct

When I invest money in something, I want to get the most I can for every dollar I spend.

Buying a car

Several years ago I purchased a new car. I went into the dealership and picked out the model and color, I looked at the sticker price on the window and wrote a check to the dealer for the full amount. Wrong! I did **not** write a check for the sticker price.

My wife and I have been married for over 30 years and she has learned not to go to the car dealer when I am ready to buy. Her blood pressure cannot take the negotiating that I do.

Years ago my father told me something that I have never forgotten. I am sure that you have heard this expression as well: *Buy low and sell high.* The only time that people do not apply this instinct is with their investments. When we buy a house, a car, shop for clothes or food, we look for the best deals we can get.

(CD) The traditional model of investing for retirement

Typically, when you start saving for retirement, the traditional model indicates that you should be aggressively invested when you are young. Then, as you reach middle age, you should be more moderately aggressive. As you approach your late fifties, your investments should be moderately conservative. When you reach retirement age a large portion of your money should be conservatively invested.

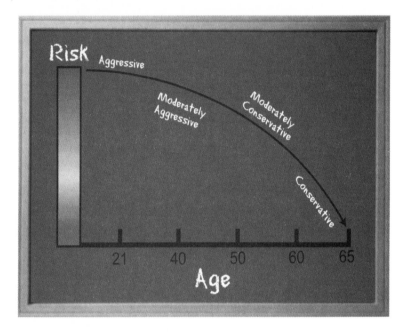

For most people, this traditional model has one **fatal flaw** – it assumes that you will have enough money for retirement. Since most people with whom I work will not have enough saved for retirement, using the *Sell High Model* allows you to be more aggressively invested for a longer period of time.

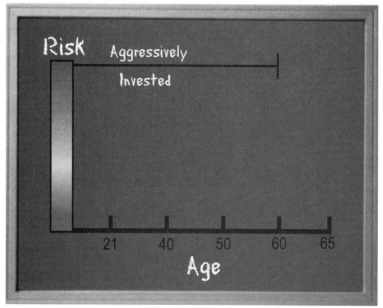

By staying more aggressively invested in the market throughout your retirement life, you can increase your chances of having more money when you are old.

Building up a *stash of cash* before you retire can allow you to weather the ups and downs of the market. This stash of cash becomes your **retirement cash reserves** to help make up the shortfall between your retirement income and expenses. Most importantly, if the market is down, your stash buys you time for the market to come back up.

This stash will insulate you from the ups and downs of the market. It is your cushion of protection, giving you time to make decisions.

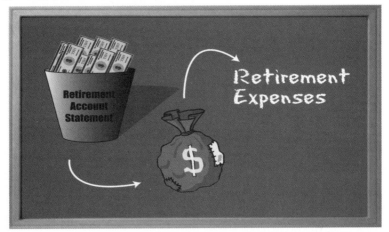

If the economy really looks lousy you have time to rethink how you are spending your retirement dollars. Do you need two cars, do you need a second home, or do you have to take three cruises a year? This cushion of time given to you by your stash creates an opportunity for you to review your finances without having to panic when the market is down.

The Sell High Model puts you in charge of managing your shares for retirement.

Chapter 11

(CD) When I Pick Out Mutual Funds

There are as many ways to pick mutual funds as there are planners and advisors. I suggest you find a financial professional to help you with this decision.

When I pick out mutual funds I do not put all of my eggs in one basket.

I put 20% of my investment money in small size companies, 30% in medium size companies, and 50% in large companies. Large companies are my base. Since small companies are riskier I put less money into them.

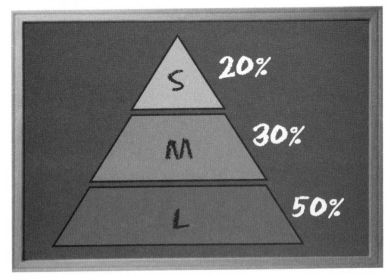

Throwing mud on the wall

Picking a mutual fund is a little like scientifically throwing mud on the wall – you can look at past performance and other indicators, however, **no one** can tell you what the fund will be doing 10, 20, or 30 years from now.

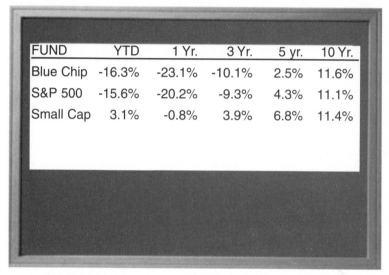

FUND	YTD	1 Yr.	3 Yr.	5 yr.	10 Yr.
Blue Chip	-16.3%	-23.1%	-10.1%	2.5%	11.6%
S&P 500	-15.6%	-20.2%	-9.3%	4.3%	11.1%
Small Cap	3.1%	-0.8%	3.9%	6.8%	11.4%

Nobody knows the future.

The key to investing is to remember that you are buying: the more you buy, the more you will have to sell.

Gas stove

To me, retirement is like a huge gas stove with all of the burners turned up. On the stove are pots of money. Each pot represents a different mutual fund in which you are invested.

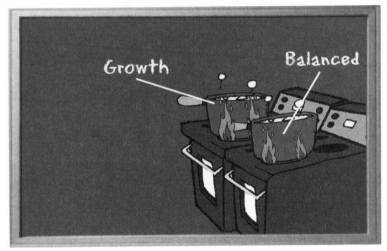

You are only going to take money from the pots that are boiling the most – that's the **Sell High** model concept. The problem you are faced with is that no one knows what will be boiling when you are ready to retire.

I try to pick funds that if the economy is up the funds are up. These are typically called *growth* funds. I also try to pick funds that if the economy is down the funds are up. These are typically called *value* funds. I want to try to increase my chances that something will be boiling when I get ready to retire.

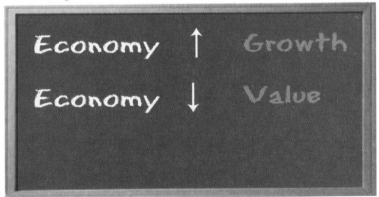

So in my small size companies, I want a growth fund and a value fund. In my medium size companies, I want a growth fund and a value fund and in my large size companies, I want a growth fund and a value fund. I want one of each (growth and value) in my different size companies because *no one knows* what will be boiling when I retire.

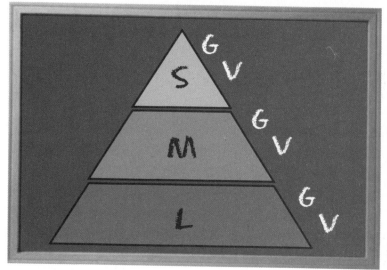

Common sense makes sense. The more pots you have on the stove the higher your chance that one will be boiling.

Chapter 12

The Difference Between Growth and Value Funds

Growth fund managers look for consistent performance. Value fund managers look for out of favor companies.

Growth Fund

Growth fund managers buy shares of stock in companies that are doing well and reporting higher profits each year. As an example, if you were a growth fund manager and one of your research assistants reported to you that Microsoft has a 5 year track record of a 10% annual return, then you might purchase shares of Microsoft for your fund based on that 5 year history of growth and the anticipated growth.

Value Fund

Value fund managers buy shares of stock in companies that are underperforming or are out of favor with the market. In this case, your research assistant might tell you about IBM.

At one time, IBM was the monster in the computer industry. Almost every large company in the United States had IBM mainframe computers. Stories were spreading about a new company starting to manufacture personal computers. Why would anyone want a computer in their home? They are difficult to program. They take up so much space. So IBM kept making mainframes. Once PC's started becoming popular the price of IBM stock began to fall. The investor who paid $84 per share bailed out when it fell to $64. As stories were written about how IBM might go out of business, fear drove the prices down further.

When the price reached $18, your value fund research assistant might report that she had been to IBM headquarters in Chicago and found that IBM had the cash to develop smaller computers. They had the research and development departments to make the switch to PC's and they had the manufacturing capabilities to make the new computers. As the value fund manager you could buy at $18 a share and ride the greed curve up.

If you have growth funds and value funds in your retirement plan, you are increasing your chances that something will be boiling when you retire.

Chapter 13

Reallocate or Sell All?

Should I Reallocate My Existing Funds?

When you reallocate or rebalance, you *sell* some or all of your existing shares and purchase new shares in the funds you selected. If the market is down you are selling *low*.

You may be purchasing new shares at low prices if you are buying the same type of funds. However, rather than trying to pick funds that will outperform the ones you already own, consider leaving your existing funds on the stove and pick new funds in which to start purchasing shares. Instead of selling shares you already own, just change your *future investments* to new funds.

Should I Sell All of My Shares at Once?

Remember the stove. Imagine you are in your 3 to 5 year window before retirement. You are watching your pots and now something is boiling (the price of one of your funds hits its highest price). If you were to sell all of your shares you would be taking that pot off of the stove. However, if you sold just some of your shares, that pot would still be on the stove. It may boil even more later (the prices may be going up) – and later could be 5 or 10 years from now.

When you take a pot off the stove you start to lose your diversification. All of your eggs could wind up in one basket. I prefer to leave some of my shares in my pots to sell at a later date. That way, after I retire, I can have 20 or 30 more years to sell.

Suppose the economy is booming and I am in the 3 to 5 year window before my retirement. I have determined that I need $10,000 for my stash of cash. When one of my funds hits its highest price I might only take out $2000. I will then wait a little while to see if the price goes higher. If it does I would sell fewer shares to get the next $2000. The fewer shares I sell, the longer my shares will last. However, *I am not going to wait* to see how high it will go.

I want to start building up my stash *no matter what* is going on in the economy. If I am in my 3 to 5 year window and the market is down, then I will change my future investments so 100% of my contributions go directly into the Guaranteed Interest Account. *I want to make sure I have money in my stash before I retire.*

Chapter 14
Do I Have My Money in "Good" Funds?

Most mutual funds are "good" funds. If they are in your retirement plan, chances are your plan has an investment committee which reviews the performance of the mutual funds to make sure they meet the plan's performance criteria. It's tough to say that one fund is better than another because no one can predict how the funds will do in the future. In fact, in every mutual fund prospectus you will find words to the effect that *"past performance is not a guarantee of future results."* No one knows the future.

When you select a mutual fund you have a professional manager(s) and a research department working for you. They are the first people to know that there is a problem when their fund is not performing well. They also have the resources to correct the problem. Instead of working eight hour days, they are working twelve hour days to fix that problem. You usually will not discover that the fund prices are down or that the performance is off until you get your statement months later. Deciding to get out of that fund means you are second guessing a professional manager with a research department.

When I do not like the way one of my funds is performing, I pick a new fund to replace it. But, I do not sell the shares I have in that fund because 10 or

20 years from now that may be the pot that is boiling. *I only change my future investments to a new fund or funds.*

Let's play bridge!

Several years ago I worked with a retired couple in their early 80's. They asked me to sell them some mutual funds. I reviewed their current financial position and found that they had over $1 million dollars in Certificates of Deposit. When asked why they wanted mutual funds, they indicated that every time they met with their bridge group their partners would be talking about their mutual funds and they didn't have anything to talk about. I explained to them that the next time they were playing bridge they should look over at each other and be glad they didn't have to take risks like that because they had enough money to last them throughout retirement.

Retirement is really easy. If you have enough money you can quit at any time. But, to be conservatively invested, you need to have a lot of money.

Typically, bond funds are considered conservative investments. Most asset allocation models or portfolio optimization models include a portion of your investments in bonds or CD-like investments.

If you are buying a house, you are most probably paying more for your mortgage than you are contributing to your retirement plan. If you think about it, you are already investing a lot of money each month in something conservative. Your house usually goes up in value every year, so the investment choices you make for your retirement plan could be more aggressive.

Most people will not have enough money to retire the way they originally imagined. Being more aggressively invested may mean you could have more money for retirement.

Bad things make good

Almost daily we read or hear about some scandal, corruption or violation of the law in the business world. Sometimes this news can rock the stock market. Scandals such as Enron, Worldcom and others will continue to affect people's attitudes about investing in the stock market. However, when something bad happens that does not mean it will be bad forever.

Since the Enron and Worldcom scandals, we will have safer and better accounting standards in the future. After the dotcom crash we have a new group of fund managers who took the wild ride and know that there are consequences for their actions. I believe this leads to a stronger market because we can count on better accounting and more seasoned managers. *We can get some good out of the bad.*

Chapter 15

Taking Calculated Risks

Are you conservative?

Most people I meet with tell me they are conservative and do not want to take risks. If you have ever completed an Investment Risk Tolerance questionnaire you found that you are conservative or moderately conservative. I have yet to meet the person who tells me that I can do whatever I want to with their money. You are conservative – not a risk taker.

However, most people I meet drive cars. Think of the risks you take every day on the road. The reason we do not let the risk stop us is that we have been driving for a while, we are familiar with our route to and from work, we know the best times to travel and we keep our cars in good shape. The reason we do not want to take risks with our money is because we do not understand the stock market or how mutual funds work. Nobody wants to end up without money for retirement.

When we drive our cars we take *calculated risks*. We should do the same thing with our retirement planning. Make sure you look at the long term performance of the mutual funds, review their objectives and learn enough about how things work to make informed decisions about investing. I have never asked anyone to calculate the beta of a mutual fund. I *do* ask them to keep track of the highest price they paid for their shares and to control when they sell them. ***By gaining an understanding of investing you can take greater risks because they are calculated risks.***

Can I lose all of my money?

Yes, you could lose all of your money, ***but***, chances are that will not happen. When you invest your money in mutual funds you have a professional manager or management team with a research department. These people are buying and selling every day. Additionally, when you choose different mutual funds with different investment objectives, you are not putting all of your eggs in one basket.

If one of your funds is the S&P 500 Stock Index fund, your fund has almost all of the top 500 companies in the United States in its portfolio. When you wake up tomorrow and listen to the morning news, you learn that WALMART, General Motors, AT&T, IBM and Ford all went out of business last night. Your mutual fund still has shares from the 495 companies that did not go out of business. And if all of those large companies did go out of business all at once, we would have more worries than how our retirement funds were looking.

One Hundred Economists

If the market was down and there were one hundred economists in the same room, no two of them would agree on when the market would come back up. However, *all of them* would agree that it will come back.

The longest period that the market has been down since World War II (using the S&P 500 Index as a reference) was 70 months from October, 1974 until July, 1980. No one knows when the market will come back up, but, it will come back up.

We are about to embark on the largest wealth transfer in the history of the world. More money is going to flow through inheritances than at any other time. Unlike our parents or grandparents who saved, we are going to spend. The global economy will have hiccups but it cannot be stopped. *The unknown is WHEN not IF*.

Year-to-Date Return (YTD)

One day I looked at one of my accounts online and saw that my year-to-date (YTD) return was 22.3%. Since the market has historically averaged 10%, most people would be excited about having a 22.3% return. I do not get real excited and here is why.

Every payday I am buying shares. Year-to-date means from the beginning of the year (January) until now (the current date). If I was paying $10 per share in January, I am now paying $12.23 for the same share (which is 22.3% higher). I am not getting as many shares for my money, am I?

This is a little like going to the grocery store and having the checkout clerk tell you that you owe $10 for your purchases. You reach into your wallet or purse and tell him that you want to give him $12.23

because $10 is not enough! Getting excited about the market being up is good if you are selling. However, while you are working you are buying – lower prices mean you are buying more.

The market goes up or down each day. The one thing you can count on for certain is that your number of shares is increasing because you are buying them.

Chapter 16

CD Investing for Retirement

Investing for retirement is different than investing for other goals.

Most of the articles you read and most of the shows on television talk about making money **NOW**. Retirement planning is for the **future**.

At forty years of age, you still have almost fifty more years to live. Fifty years is a long time to have money in mutual funds. If you manage your money in retirement you have the ability to use time to control when you sell. You cannot control the prices of your shares, but you can control when you sell them.

Don't forget that you are looking at a twenty to thirty year time frame, even after retirement, to watch prices and wait for the highest price.

The news covers what is happening *today.* Your retirement is based on a long term perspective. ***Keep long term in mind***.

Chapter 17

Employer Plans and How They are Taxed

CD **What is tax deferral?**
When you reach into your wallet or pocketbook and pull out a $20 bill, you had to earn $26 to get that $20 bill. Where did the $6 go? Uncle Sam gets the $6 in taxes. He gets these taxes every time you get a paycheck.

Retirement plans are *tax deferred*. To defer means to "put off" or "to postpone." The government allows us to postpone paying taxes on the money that we put into our retirement plan.

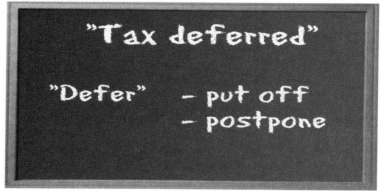

We can put off paying the taxes until we take the money out in retirement.

Uncle Sam says that if you contribute $20 into your retirement plan, you do not have to pay the $6 in taxes now. He lets you take the $6 you would have paid in taxes and add that to the $20 you contributed from your paycheck. In essence, you are investing $26 per payday even though only $20 comes out of your paycheck.

Before taxes and after taxes

You have heard people speaking of before taxes and after taxes. The $26 is "before" taxes and the $20 is "after" taxes.

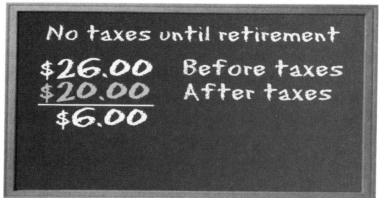

You can be making a $26 contribution to your retirement plan while your take home pay will only be reduced by $20. The government can afford to wait for us to pay the taxes because it outlives all of us.

Tax deferral allows you to save not only the $20 that is taken out of your paycheck but also the $6 you would have paid in taxes as well. This additional money compounded over time means you can accumulate more for retirement.

If you earn $25,000 this year and you contribute $2000 to your retirement plan, at the end of the year your W-2 will show that you only earned $23,000. You were able to deduct the $2000 from your taxable income. You will have to pay taxes on $23,000. You are deferring paying taxes on the $2000 until you take the money out at retirement.

What is a tax shelter?

Think of the money that you are putting into your retirement plan and the money your employer is putting in as going into a big bubble. Uncle Sam does not tax the money inside the bubble (it is sheltered) because you and he want it to grow as big as possible. Can you guess why? When you take the money out in retirement it becomes income to you and you get to pay income taxes on what you take out each year. Uncle Sam gets paid when you retire.

As long as it is inside the tax shelter bubble, you are allowed to move your money around as much as you like. You can make changes between funds, sell shares of funds and move the money to a Guaranteed Interest Account without any tax consequences. However, when you take it out, Uncle Sam gets paid before you do. Most retirement plans are required to take out 20% for taxes before they send the money to you. This means that if you want $1000 you need to ask for $1250 because they will send $250 (20% x $1250) to the IRS and the $1000 to you.

When you do your taxes at the end of the year the IRS knows that you already paid taxes on that money so you do not have to pay taxes twice. There is no tax free money in a retirement plan – only tax deferred and tax sheltered. *Uncle Sam always gets paid!*

What is the difference between a 401(k) and a 403(b)?

Think of the IRS Tax Code as chapters in the Bible. Chapter 401 has verses a, b, c,...k, etc. Chapter

401 regulates retirement plans that are for the most part in for-profit companies, such as General Motors, IBM, and WALMART.

The rules which govern a 401(k) are a little different than the rules for a 403(b). Chapter 403 also has verses a,b,c, etc. and it regulates the retirement plans for most not-for-profit or non-profit companies and organizations. A church-based hospital would have a 403(b).

Additionally, some employees are covered by Chapter 457. This chapter regulates government organizations such as county, public school or state plans. It is usually referred to as a Deferred Compensation Plan. There is a verse in Chapter 457 which allows employers to offer an additional way of saving by using tax deferred dollars. If you are already contributing the maximum to your 403(b), you could save more if your employer offers the Deferred Compensation Plan. This plan is not available to all employers, so check with your Human Resources department to see if it is available where you work.

There is some overlap in how the plans can be used by different businesses. As Congress seeks to make retirement plans easier to understand, many of the distinctions that once existed are starting to go away. Changes in the tax legislation have created the Simple IRA and the Simple 401(k) plans. They all work much the same in that they have tax deferral and tax shelter provisions. The amounts the employer and employee can contribute vary according to each plan. Plan provisions are always changing as Congress tries to make them more attractive to encourage saving for retirement.

How does a defined contribution plan work?

Most retirement plans today are defined contribution plans. This means *you define the contribution* you wish to make. Some employers contribute a *basic percentage* like 3% or 4% of your salary. This money does not come from your paycheck. Your employer contributes this in addition to what you're being paid.

Other employers contribute money only if you put in some money of your own. This provision is called a *match*. Some employers do both the basic percentage and a match.

Employer basic and match

Let's say your employer puts in a basic contribution of 3 percent of your pay. If you earn $30,000 a year, your employer would add $900 (3% x $30,000) to your retirement plan; and if your employer matches your contribution 50% of the first 4% you contribute, your employer will put in an additional 2% of your salary (50% of 4%). In this example, if you earn $30,000 a year and you contribute $1200 (4% x $30,000); your employer will put in an additional $600 (2% x $30,000). The $600 match is like giving yourself almost a $.30 per hour raise just by participating in the plan.

Match money is **free money**. If you put in $1200, your employer will put in an additional $600. There is no bank or credit union you can walk into and hand them $1200 and they will immediately write you a check for $600. But that is exactly what happens in your retirement plan. This is a guaranteed 50% return on your investment.

Your total investment toward retirement would be the employer basic of $900, your voluntary contribution of $1200, and the $600 match or a total of $2700 each year.

Vesting

Employers who make basic and matching contributions usually put a condition on the money they put in towards your retirement. That condition is called *vesting*.

Some retirement plans have a 5 year *cliff* vesting schedule. This means that you must work for the same employer for 5 years before you are fully vested. Only then will the employer contributions be yours to keep.

Other plans have a *stepped and graded* schedule which varies with the number of years you work for your employer. With this type of vesting schedule, you might be eligible for 20% of the money your employer contributed after you have worked for them for 2 years. After your third year you could keep 40% of their contribution. To get the full 100% employer contribution, you would need to work for the company for 6 years. At that time, all of the money your employer contributed would be yours.

Your Money (Voluntary Contributions)

You are always fully vested in the money you contribute to your retirement plan. If you leave employment before you are vested, the employer gets the money they contributed returned to them, but you still get to keep the money you have contributed. *If your company offers a retirement plan it makes sense to participate.*

What is a defined benefit plan?

Think of the words: they *define* the *benefit*. If you worked at the same company for 15, 20, or 30 years, you could get a defined benefit in the form of a guaranteed monthly income for the rest of your life. Your benefit (monthly check) depends on the number of years you worked at the company. It is usually computed using your last 3 or 5 years' salary and your estimated life expectancy. This type of plan is still common among state and county employers and will continue to provide benefits to employees for many years to come.

Often, when I meet with clients who work in a school system or serve in the military, most of them are concerned about the small amount of money they have been able to save for retirement.

I show them this example. Suppose your pension would be $1000 per month or $12,000 per year. Personally, I am not eligible for a defined benefit pension plan because I have never worked for an employer who provided that kind of benefit. So I would need to have money saved up on my own to give me that $1000 per month. If interest rates were 4%, I would need to have saved $300,000 to get $12,000 ($300,000 x 4%) per year. I would need to save a lot of money to have the same benefit. Even though they cannot call up their pension plan and ask them for the $300,000, it works the same as if they had saved up the money in their retirement plan. If you have a defined benefit plan, you have more than you think.

If you do have a defined benefit plan, you will need to elect your benefit when you retire. You can usually choose to have your benefit paid out over your lifetime, over your lifetime and your spouse's lifetime, or some combination of the above. *Once you make this choice it is permanent and cannot be changed. Make sure you completely understand your options before you sign for the benefit.*

Chapter 18

CD How Can I Start to Save for Retirement?

Crawl, Walk and Run

As a minimum goal, you should be saving 10% of your pay for retirement.

Most people are already up to their ears with bills and are just trying to keep afloat. You already have your family budget established so rather than trying to put in 10% of your pay immediately, I suggest that you start slowly and work your way up.

The easiest way for you to start putting money into your retirement plan is to put in your raises. This is how you learn to *crawl*. Perhaps you will get a 2% raise this year. Put that 2% into your retirement plan. Next year, if you put in your next 2% raise, you would be saving a total of 4% of your pay. You will not miss having that 4% of your pay because you never had it to spend.

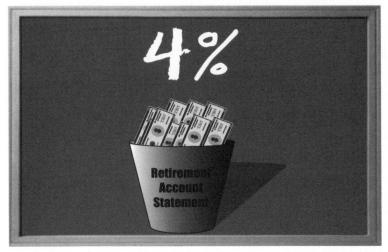

Now you can start to *walk*. Once you are contributing the amount you need to get the employer match, start splitting your raises with the plan. For example, if you get a 3% raise put 2% in for retirement and keep 1% for yourself.

Next year, you could keep 2% for yourself and put in 1% for retirement. Keep splitting raises and before long you will be saving 10% of your pay.

The *run* part of saving usually starts after your children have graduated from high school or college and you no longer have the expenses of raising a family. Since you do not have much time left to invest, you should be trying to save as much as you can. *Remember, the money you will have for retirement is money that you have saved. The more you put in now, the more you will have later.*

Chapter 19

Can I Put a Lump Sum of Money Into My Retirement Plan?

Tax Refund

Doris just got her tax refund. She has a 401(k) at work and wants to put the refund money into her retirement plan. Can she do it? The answer is yes, as long as Doris does not exceed the IRS contribution limits.

Doris' refund was $1000. She deposited the $1000 into her checking account. She could then increase her contribution to her retirement plan an extra $100 per pay period for the next 10 paydays. Since her paycheck would then be $100 short, she could take any extra money she needed out of her checking account.

Once the $1000 from her checking account has been used up, she would change her contribution back to the original amount she was contributing. This technique works for money you might have saved for retirement – CDs, an inheritance, or extra savings.

Can I put money into my retirement plan even though I have terminated employment?

While you were working you were participating in your employer plan. You were making contributions to the retirement plan every payday from your paycheck. Since you are no longer an employee, you are no longer receiving a paycheck. You cannot contribute to the plan. Only current employees can contribute to an employer plan.

After terminating employment, you keep the vested portion of your retirement account. Usually, you have an opportunity to rollover your money into an IRA, to keep your retirement account, or to rollover to your new employer plan. Each plan has its own rules. Check with your plan administrator to find out your options.

Chapter 20

Should I Rollover My Former Employer Retirement Account?

The standard answer is yes. I personally, however, do not get really excited about rolling over money because *any time you roll or move or transfer money, you are selling.* If the market is down that means you would be selling low. Since this book is about selling high, you can see my dilemma. Selling low does not excite me. Ultimately, it is your decision.

In some circumstances it may make sense to rollover or transfer funds from one plan to another. It may make sense to roll money into more aggressive funds if you are in conservative funds and have a long time until retirement. It may also make sense to move your money if you can get a higher rate of interest on your stash of cash in the Guaranteed Interest Account. Just make sure you fully understand the implications of rolling or transferring from one plan to another. Sometimes there are surrender charges and other fees that may be charged.

In some instances, you will be forced to move your money. If a plan terminates or if your balance is less than certain limits, you may be forced to sell your shares and put the money into an IRA or another employer plan.

I prefer to think of the money in former employer plans as pots on the stove. If I keep them, I will have more chances that something will be boiling when I get ready to retire. Maybe, just maybe, one of the pots I was going to rollover will be at its highest price when I am in my 3 to 5 year window before retirement – no one knows! *I like a lot of pots on the stove.*

Chapter 21

Are IRAs Better?

You decide. There are two kinds of retirement IRAs.

Traditional IRA

The Traditional IRA was designed to provide tax deductibility and tax deferral. You can deduct the money you contribute to your IRA from your taxes and you do not have to pay taxes on any increase until you take the money out at retirement. Sounds a little like your retirement plan at work, doesn't it? However, there is a provision in the tax code which makes the tax deductibility go away if you earn too much income.

With the traditional IRA you may not be able to deduct all of your contribution. The deductibility amounts change each year so if you are contributing to a Traditional IRA, make sure you check the limits. Just ask the financial services company which has your IRA or talk with your tax advisor.

Also, remember that when you take your money out at retirement, you will have to pay income taxes on the amount you receive since it becomes income to you just like in your employer retirement plan.

Roth IRA

The Roth IRA works a little differently. There is

no tax deduction for the contributions you make to the Roth. You are using after-tax dollars to contribute to the IRA – that means that when you write the check for your Roth IRA you have already paid taxes on the money you are contributing. The growth accumulates tax deferred just like the traditional IRA, but when you take money out of the Roth IRA you do not have to pay any taxes on it. At that point it is *tax free*.

There is probably a place in your retirement portfolio for an IRA. Choosing which IRA would work best for you depends upon your income and what you want it to do for you. However, your first choice should always be to contribute to your employer's plan, especially if it has a match.

Maximum contribution limits

All retirement savings plans have maximum limits for contributions. These limits change. I have made no attempt to address this issue since this information would be available to you from your plan administrator, plan website, or the company with whom you are investing.

Chapter 22

What is Catch-Up?

If you have worked for the same employer for fifteen years or more and you are contributing to a 403(b), also called a Tax Sheltered or Tax Deferred Annuity (TSA/TDA), you may be eligible for an IRS Tax Code provision called **Catch-Up**. This is **in addition** to the standard maximum contribution limits. It allows you to contribute up to an additional $3000 per year for a total of $15,000. Uncle Sam has this provision to allow employees who were not able to contribute as much money toward retirement as they would have liked when they were raising children and had the expenses of a family to catch-up.

Think of Catch-Up as an adding machine where you add up dollars. You can put up to $3000 dollars a year on the machine. Let's say you put in $3000 for the first year so the total on the adding machine shows $3000. Next year, if you contribute $3000, the total on the adding machine is now $6000. The following year you can only afford to contribute $2000 so the third year total is now $8000. You can continue doing this until the adding machine totals $15,000.

Once you reach the total of $15,000 you cannot contribute any more to Catch-Up. You must now use the standard maximum contribution limits. Remember, to use this provision of the Tax Code, you must be contributing the standard maximum limit already and must be employed by the same employer for fifteen years. These provisions are also subject to change so check with your plan administrator to make sure you have current information.

Chapter 23

I Need Money—Should I Take Out a Loan from My Retirement Plan?

Most retirement plans have a loan provision. If you have a loan provision, the rules for the loan features vary from plan to plan. Check with your plan administrator to see what your company plan offers.

Usually, you can get a general purpose loan which would be paid back in a period of 1 to 5 years or a loan to purchase a principal residence which would have a longer payback period like 10 to 15 years. If you borrow from your account, the plan may charge the same interest rate as the Guaranteed Account rate. What they do is take the amount of money that you are borrowing and pay you interest at the guaranteed rate. They then charge you interest at the same rate on the amount you borrow. This makes the net interest rate on your loan – zero. For example, if your guaranteed rate is 6%, you will be paid 6% interest and you will be charged 6% interest, so your net interest is zero.

Some companies charge a one or more percent difference which means that you will be paying a little more for your loan than in the above example. They may charge 8% while paying you 6% on the amount you borrow. You get a great deal because you can get a loan for zero or two percent. The banks and credit unions cannot match that interest rate. Your plan may also have a loan processing fee which helps cover the cost of administering the loan.

The catch

When you sign up for your loan, you will be asked for payroll information or debit information so the payments can be taken from your paycheck or bank.

The IRS sets limits on the amount you can borrow. The maximum limit is 50% of the balance in your account up to $50,000. If you have $10,000 in your account, you can borrow 50% of the amount or $5000. For example, your daughter needs braces and you want to borrow the money from your retirement plan. You have $10,000 in your account and need to borrow $4000. You call up your retirement plan service center and make arrangements for the loan. Your monthly payments are $75.

Every month the $75 will be taken from your bank account or your paycheck. In order for you to have $75 to make the payment you actually had to earn more than that because you had to pay taxes on the money. You are making payments to your retirement account using *after-tax* dollars.

You have paid back your loan and years later you retire and start taking money from your stash to pay your retirement expenses. When you take money from your stash you will have to pay income taxes because the taxes were deferred. You will be paying taxes *again* on the money you paid back. You will be paying taxes *TWICE*.

Default on loan

If you stop making payments and your loan defaults, you may be subject to an Early Withdrawal Penalty. If you are under 59$1/2$ and you default, you are required to pay a 10% Early Withdrawal Penalty for the balance of the loan. Let's say you borrowed $4000 and before you could make the first payment, your spouse lost her job. You can't make the payments. When the loan defaults, the $4000 becomes taxable income to you – you have to pay income taxes. If you are under 59$1/2$ you would also have to pay the 10% penalty. If you are in the 20% tax bracket, it would cost you $400 ($4000 x 10%) for the Early Withdrawal penalty and $800 ($4000 x 20%) for income taxes. That means you paid $1200 ($400 + $800) in penalties and taxes to get $4000. When you do your taxes at the end of the year you owe Uncle Sam an extra $1200. Paying $1200 to get $4000 is not a deal. If you are over 59$1/2$, you would not have to pay the 10% penalty. You would still have to pay the taxes.

Use the loan feature carefully. This could be some of the most expensive money you can borrow. I suggest that you use this as a last resort – when you cannot get money from any other source.

What's magic about 59 $1/2$?

Uncle Sam lets us save money without paying taxes on it in our retirement plans. He allows us to do this since we are saving for retirement. If we want to use that money for something other than retirement, he has rules about taking it out. His magic number is 59½. If you are under that age and take out money – you pay the 10% Early Withdrawal Penalty illustrated above. If you are over 59½, you don't have to pay the penalty. However, you will always have to pay income taxes on it since it was before-tax money.

The IRS Tax Code provides some situations where you can withdraw money from your retirement account without the penalty. Some plans allow you to take out a hardship withdrawal, pay for a college education, pay for unforeseen medical expenses or purchase a principal residence. You need to check with your plan administrator for the specifics. In each instance, you will still need to pay the income taxes since you took the money out.

Chapter 24

What Is a Required Minimum Distribution (RMD)?

Uncle Sam allows us to save money tax deferred until we reach 70^1/$_2$ and then he *requires* us to start taking out some of the money we have saved in our retirement plan. His reason is simple – he wants to make sure we pay taxes on all the money we have saved before we die.

When we take out the money it becomes income to us and he gets the taxes we pay on the income. We don't have to take all of the money out, only a portion each year. This is called the Required Minimum Distribution. Uncle Sam's plan is that if your estimated life expectancy is 26 years after 70^1/$_2$, you would be required to take out 1/26th of the amount each year so that at the end of the 26 years all of the money is taxed.

There are Required Minimum Distribution tables and formulas that give you the minimum amount you must take each year as a distribution. Usually the retirement plan company will notify you that you have to take out the amount and will send you paperwork to get your RMD. If you are working at 70^1/$_2$ you do not have to take a RMD from your retirement plan until you quit working. However, if you have an IRA, you are required to take distributions at 70^1/$_2$. These rules are always subject to change so check with your retirement plan company to make sure you have current information about the RMD.

CD **Using the enclosed CD**
As you look at what mutual funds are and how they work, you may want to use the enclosed CD to help you follow the concepts discussed. The CD is a multimedia presentation to let you actually see how the numbers on the tables develop and to show the flow of the discussion. If you see the "CD" symbol with the title of the topic, you will find that material on the enclosed CD.

For Windows users: Insert CD; CD will auto-run

For Macintosh users: Insert CD; Open the files through your browser

Afterword

I hope you've enjoyed the material and examples. My wish is that you now have a clearer understanding about how your decisions can affect your retirement.

The examples I've used – 3 to 5 years before I retire to start watching share prices and having a 3 year stash of cash are time frames I personally have chosen. I understand that everyone's financial situation is different and that you are going to need to choose time frames that make sense to you.

At one of my presentations, a participant said that he wanted to start looking 7 years before he retired and he wanted to have 7 years worth of money in his stash. I told him that was fine because it was his money. Now, at least he has a framework from which to make decisions.

May your decisions about your retirement be wiser because of the understanding you have learned through reading this book.

Remember, know how much you paid and sell high.

Glossary

Account Value – your balance; number on your statement which tells you how much money you have; changes daily based on share prices

After Taxes – money you have after you pay the taxes

Aggressive – the way most people should invest; typically assumes a higher degree of risk; has potential for more money

Asset – something you buy and something you can sell; your shares; sell for at least as much as you paid for them

Asset Allocation – what you do when you pick out different mutual funds; method used by financial professionals to apply scientific principles to mutual fund selection

Average Share Cost – all of the money you paid for your shares divided by all the shares you bought

Basic Contribution – a contribution which the employer makes to a retirement plan

Before Taxes – money you have before any taxes are paid; the gross pay on your paycheck

Bond Fund – typically considered a conservative investment

Beta – a calculation which measures how closely a mutual fund performance varies from a benchmark index; for example, if the beta of a mutual fund is 1.0, it matches the index exactly; if it is .5, it could range from 50% to 150% of the index

Calculated Risk – something we take every day; if we understand what we are doing we can be more in control

Catch-Up – what you can do if you have worked for the same employer for at least 15 years and are over 50; the rules are subject to change so make sure you get current information

Conservative – the way most people feel they should invest; typically generates a lower return on your investment; balanced funds, bond funds, guaranteed interest accounts

Diversification – not all of your eggs in one basket

Defined Benefit Plan – a pension plan that pays a specific benefit over a specific time or lifetime; the employer defines the benefit

Defined Contribution Plan – a retirement plan in which you define the contribution, the amount of money you are going to put in

Dollar Cost Averaging – what you are doing by putting money into your retirement plan when you have money taken from your paycheck; you are buying as prices go up and down

Early Withdrawal Penalty – a 10% penalty you pay on retirement savings that you withdraw before age 59$^1/_2$

Employer Match – additional money some employers contribute to your retirement plan if you voluntarily put in some money of your own

Equity – another word for "stock"

Gas Stove – where you have your mutual funds (pots) and what you watch when you get ready to retire

Growth Fund – a mutual fund with growth as an objective; fund manager looks for growth potential in companies the fund purchases

Guaranteed Interest Account – a stable value fund which pays a guaranteed interest rate for a specific period of time; like a Certificate of Deposit for one year or a different time frame

Individual Retirement Agreement (IRA) – a tax qualified arrangement which acts like a retirement plan; has lower contribution limits than retirement plans

Losing Money – what you would do if you panicked and sold your shares when the market is down; only happens if you actually move, transfer, or sell

Market Timing – waiting until the market is at a low point and then buying shares low; works about 2% of the time; not real good odds

Maximum Contribution Limits – the maximum amount you can contribute to your retirement plan; these limits change every year

Mutual Fund – a professionally managed collection of shares in companies bought and sold to achieve a financial objective; a manager or management team has a research department to figure out what to buy and what to sell; places to put money for investing; pots on the stove

Plan Administrator – usually someone in your Human Resources or Personnel department

Reallocate – taking the money you currently have invested and investing it in a new way; selling your shares and buying shares in new mutual funds

Rebalance – figuring out which of your mutual funds are doing well and selling some of those shares to buy shares in the funds you have which are not doing well

Required Minimum Distribution (RMD) – a minimum amount you are required to take out of your retirement accounts once you reach $70^{1}/_{2}$

Rollover – typically taking money you have in a retirement account with a FORMER employer and putting it into your retirement account with your CURRENT employer; you can also take from a FORMER employer plan and put it in an IRA

Roth IRA – an IRA which allows you to put money in from your checking or savings account on an after tax basis; the growth is not taxed when you take it out

Sell (Move, Transfer, Roll) – what you do when you take your money and change what you do with it

Share – a part of the mutual fund in which you are investing; something you buy when you give your money to a financial advisor or your retirement plan; something you can sell; your asset

Share Price – what you paid to purchase a share; prices change daily and are calculated at the close of the market (at the end of each day)

Small, Medium, Large – refers to size of the companies in which fund managers invest; usually called Small Cap, Mid-Cap, and Large Cap

Stash of Cash – money invested in a Guaranteed Interest Account; like a cash reserve from which you take money to live on in retirement and to which you put money from selling your shares

Tax Deferral – putting off paying taxes for a while

Tax Free – exists only in your imagination; Uncle Sam always gets paid – either now or later

Tax Shelter – putting off paying taxes until you take out the money; your money is sheltered (protected) from taxes until you get it

Traditional IRA – an IRA which allows you to make before tax contributions if you meet the income tests; you can deduct contributions from your income as long as you qualify; taxed when you take money out

Transfer – what you do when you have money in a retirement account with your CURRENT employer and you put it in a different retirement account you have with your CURRENT employer

Unit – if you have an annuity you may be buying units – treat like shares

Unit Value – if you have an annuity you may see this on your statement – treat like share price; usually written like 2.390876 (which is really $2.39); it has so many numbers because there are a lot of units (shares) in a mutual fund

Value Fund – a mutual fund whose manager looks for companies that are out of favor with the current investing climate; value funds act differently from growth funds

Vesting – who owns the money in your retirement account; if you are vested you own it; if you aren't vested the money isn't yours yet

ABOUT THE AUTHOR

Paul Pelley is a Certified Financial Planner™ Professional and a Certified Senior Advisor®. He has worked extensively in the healthcare retirement market and with government and private retirement plans.

He takes seriously the fact that most people will not have enough money saved to retire "in the fashion to which they are accustomed." He teaches how retirement plans and mutual funds work so each person can know enough about their retirement money to know what to do when they get ready to retire.

CFP® and Certified Financial Planner™ are certification marks owned by the Certified Financial Planner Board of Standards, Inc. These marks are awarded to individuals who successfully complete the CFP Board's initial and ongoing certification requirements. Use of these marks does not imply endorsement of the material contained herein.

Order Form

Give the gift of **Common Sense Retirement: How To Get MORE From Your Retirement Plan** to your children and friends.

Please send me _____ copies.

Send to:

_____
Name

_____
Address

_____
City/State/Zip

_____
Phone   E-mail

Call 1-800-765-6955 for ordering information and shipping/handling charges. Payment must accompany order. Please allow 3 weeks for delivery.

If you have any questions contact
www.MoneyManagementBooks.com

Quantity discounts are available.
Please contact distributor at 1-800-765-6955.